what my
body knows

what my body knows

LYNDA MONAHAN

COTEAU BOOKS
WWW.COTEAUBOOKS.COM

Edited by Dave Margoshes.
Cover and book design by Duncan Campbell.
Cover image, "Elemental Red: Fire," 2003, by Martha Cole.
Printed and bound in Canada at Transcontinental Printing.

National Library of Canada Cataloguing in Publication Data

Monahan, Lynda, 1952-
What my body knows / Lynda Monahan.

Poems.
ISBN 1-55050-267-0

I. Title.
PS8576.O45182W42 2003   C811'.54   C2003-911147-4

1 2 3 4 5 6 7 8 9 10

COTEAU BOOKS
401-2206 Dewdney Ave.
Regina, Saskatchewan
Canada   S4R 1H3

available in Canada and the US from:
Fitzhenry & Whiteside
195 Allstate Parkway
Markham, Ontario
Canada   L3R 4T8

The publisher gratefully acknowledges the financial assistance of the Saskatchewan Arts Board, the Canada Council for the Arts, the Government of Canada through the Book Publishing Industry Development Program (BPIDP), the Government of Saskatchewan, through the Cultural Industries Development Fund, and the City of Regina Arts Commission, for its publishing program.

for my family
then and now

watermark

these poems
hold you
in their making
like a watermark
made visible
when held to the light

table of contents

part one what my body knows

part two something worth keeping

part one

what my
body knows

when the moon slides

(david's poem)

there is nothing
i miss
quite so much
as hearing your name for me
over the phone
hearing *hi sis*

now there is nothing
but the silver charm
you gave me
for my birthday
sitting
in my jewellery box
calling me forever
by that name
            ....

they will not speak of you
will not say
it happened this way

but i won't let your dying
be for nothing

i will tell your story david
i will show them that you lived
        ....

you were born a blue baby
your skin the colour of a january sky
delicate as mother's good china
your blood the shade of delft

when we were kids
you traded me cats eyes
for the blues   you loved
them all   the milky blue-white ones
or those like sapphires
truer than any blue

and mom bringing us
to have our picture taken
all dressed up in royal blue velvet
both of us finding no reason to smile

when you were married
the hall decked with pale blue ribbons
later when she left
blue settling down around you
like her wedding veil

and when you died
in the indigo shadows
of moonlight on fallen snow
blue tingeing your lips
the fine skin over your eyes
            ....

you always lied
caught fish this big
came home covered in mud
with the story
that a rabbit
kicked dirt in your face

lied to your teacher
that dad gave you the belt
over a poor report card
she didn't realize
the welts he left
weren't on your skin

you told me once
that no one would believe
the truth

     ....

at thirteen
you took to wearing
platform shoes
tottering
on six-inch heels

longing to be tall
having always been
made small
in your father's eyes

you spent your lifetime
trying to compensate
to elevate yourself
but you could never

measure up
not ever

only in death
it seems
have you become significant
taller now
than all of us

    ....

this isn't a poem dad would say poems are for sissies and
if there's one thing he's not it's a sissy a man who's never been
to a doctor or dentist once in his life and proud of it
pulled out his own teeth with the needle-nose pliers checked
himself out of hospital the day his hand got crushed
to a pulp in the bread roller   swearing bloody hell at all
the nurses   we weren't allowed to cry   you biting
clean through your bottom lip when you broke your leg
in three places just so dad wouldn't hear you   he'd say i've
got worse'n that on the end of my nose   act like a girl
we'll put you in a damn dress   don't be a sissy   but this
isn't a poem anyway   nothing in him is poetry

  ....

it must have been a saturday
dad glued to hockey night in canada
when you shut the door
made me promise not to tell
showed me the bottle you'd bought
from rowe's rexall
with money saved
from your paper route
and over the bathroom sink
i coloured your brown hair black
you slicked it back with brylcreem
and leaning into the mirror
you asked *do i look like dad now*
i remember your eyes
needing me to say yes
the directions on the bottle
saying it was permanent

    ....

you went to kelsey
got your mechanics papers
and you fixed things
nothing you couldn't repair
make go again
dad's truck our old vw

if only
you could have
rebuilt yourself
that easily

mended what was so broken
inside of you
made everything
run right
        ....

like david
in the bible
you were
a poet/fighter
you were
his kindred spirit

had his heart

you lived as he did
fighting
the same demons

always
slinging stones
at giants
always seeking
what was true
        ....

you were saying goodbye
we did not know
you were saying it
but you were
not in so many words
but just as clearly

we thought this
nothing more
than a supper out
a gift you were giving us
but you knew
what that evening meant
a sacrament of sorts
the bread and wine

there were hints
this was goodbye
had we been paying attention
small things you said
small signs

had we been looking
we might have
seen your suffering
might have noticed you
bleeding
behind your smile

    ....

you brought it out to show us
a new green and black arctic cat
tough to handle you told us
tough to handle

on sunday a storm
swirls in from the east
you hurtle breakneck
into that white world
snow rushing at you
like stars
your heart
a throb
you cannot breathe around
hair sweatdamp
cheeks bitten
eyelashes brittle
your grip tightens
the engine surges
screams the approach to a farmyard

your last breath
silvers your beard

they say you flew
over two hundred yards
before you hit the ground
and i see you flying
your unbroken laughter
lifted on the wind
        ....

i wanted to lay blame
white-hot
into his hands
say look
this is what you've done
to your only son
this
wanted to force him
to hold it
scorching his fingers
to blackened bits of flesh
not letting him
let go
til it burned to the bone
left him branded
with the marks
of his transgression
there for everyone
to see

       ....

we shiver down
the wind-blasted street
push open
heavy glass doors
the whole family goes
not one of us
could do this alone

we are going to craig's
to buy a new pair of pants
for my brother david
a pair of black dress pants
with a thirty-six inch waist

my sister cries
when i tell the clerk
we won't need them hemmed

....

at the funeral
your favourite songs
david essex we played
rock on
just give
that old time rock 'n' roll
right up to the rafters
little brother
the old church shakin'
with these hymns
for you
forever young
the boy inside the man
    ....

when the moon
slides
down the back of the night
she treads the shadows
of tall pines
scrawls your name
on the wind
writes her grief
across the sky
in a single syllable

why?

the only answer
your name returned
from distant hills
again and again
until it fades
and there are no words
for you
at all

staring straight into the sun

(in memory of my stepmother marie carr watson)

the sympathetic doctor is there
sitting on the bed
holding your hand
in both of his
he says the words
you hardly hear

malignant
he says
brain tumours
clusters of them
you imagine dark grapes
clinging inside your skull

mrs. watson he calls you
marie you want to tell him
my name is marie
       ....

i watch you sleeping
imagine your small breath
so bitter cold
so brittle it might break
if i touched it

outside the window
the moon freezes the sky
to black lays waste
your late september lilies
in this your last garden

wind cracks through
the shivering trees
even the stars shudder
shrunken and old

everywhere this dying
silent as your sleeping
your season's hard end
        ....

now that your hair has fallen
your face reddened
by radiation
you notice
how some people
old friends among them
won't meet your eyes

they sneak glances
as if looking right at you
is too difficult
too dangerous a thing
like staring straight into the sun

they turn from you
not wanting to see
you are too painful
for their unprotected eyes

    ....

i am helping you wrap presents
on the dining room table
a confusion of coloured paper
ribbons and bows
tree lights twinkle
holiday candies red and green
in a crystal bowl

amid all these signs of celebration
you are telling me
it makes you sad
not the dying you say
it's not that
(you cut and fold
i tape and tie)

it's not knowing
if this is the last time
you will write on a little tag
merry christmas
i love you   mom
        ....

i've heard it said
that all things lost
are equal
what loss then
equals this

i am losing you

the moon's arms ache
and the wind
won't stop
its weeping
    ....

do you know
that you are beautiful
each day
you grow more beautiful
do you know that

there is a quiet grace
about you now
a tranquillity
that flows from you
soft as a memory
of moonlight over water

do you know
that you are beautiful
do you know how much you shine

....

if only i could make
something lyric for you
out of this
make it worth
a poem at least

what does it mean anyway
all this pain
if words are the most powerful drug
then marie
take all my words
i give them all gladly
if only your agony
could end

      ....

you say
if you can have
just this one summer
you will be happy
just to have this one

you talk of fishing trips
to the hanging heart lakes
sunlight like warm cider
in the august afternoon
corn roasts and barbecues
on the flower-filled deck
of your little cabin at waskesui
hummingbirds thrumming
in the pots of purple pansies
to be the first one up
in the blue sky morning

you talk of filling
buckets with fat blueberries
in the cricket heat
calling out to one another
so we won't get lost

    ....

after supper strolls
to big olaf's for ice cream
then down to the beach
to dig bare toes
in the warm sand
to watch the sun sink
over the narrows
the sky gone all crimson and gold
from king's island
the loon's call so aching
it makes you want to cry

if you can have
just this one summer
you tell me
you will be happy
just to hear once more
in the trembling aspen
the rustle of rain
coming on

one small word

*and this is how we learn to say goodbye, plucking bare words from
the language of pain – Patrick Friesen*

i visit you
out of a sense of duty
the one you gave me dad
and i sit patiently
on the plastic chair
beside your bed
in the curtained light
offer you water
from a plastic cup
but you are sleeping now

i look around me
at bleak walls
and i think there should be paintings
a monet perhaps
something to set you dreaming
but dad
you never were a dreamer
living was just as hard and real
as you could make it

whipper billy watson
you liked to call yourself
after the wrestler
and that was you
grappling your way through life
with both hands ready

and even if i hung those paintings
i know that all you'd see
would be the emptiness
that wall

   ....

you dipped us all
in the dark ink
of your anger

we scrub and scrub
still trying
to remove the stains

our hearts
still slightly cyanotic

our complexions
still faintly
tinted blue

    ....

there was always
dangling there
in the dim basement light
a deer an elk or antelope
you had shot
hung from the cobwebbed beams

always the beautiful skin
lying in soft folds
on the cement floor
the antlers on the workbench
you'd make a gunrack of

when you lifted the deer
onto the bloodstained hook
i felt myself   suspended there
          ....

you asked me once
what you did to deserve this
even morphine not touching
such monstrous pain

flesh-eating disease   the doctors told us
though it was just another name
for the anger
devouring you inches at a time
your torso half gone
the surgeons barely keeping up
to its voracity

trying so hard to beat back this horror
they sliced as fast as it grew
to save you from this killing thing
cut you right down to the bone

        ....

say something
we tell ourselves
say we cannot let you
leave like this

cannot let you go dad
with our talk so small   so empty
that it tugs in our veins
turns blue
even this brightest
of april afternoons

say we'll miss you
or we're sorry you so seldom really lived

let there be just one truth
to fill this emptiness
say something we tell ourselves
just one small word

      ....

what am i to do
with this disarray

my grieving scatters me
one moment i am contained
inside the small box of my sadness
the next i spill sorrow everywhere
for you father
for the child so full of wanting
the woman wanting still
for all that should have been

i mourn in no orderly way
know only this jumble
my tangled heart
the untidiness of loss

  ....

it meant buying two for one at the co-op
flipping through the flyers for sales
on bulk rolls of toilet paper
(even though he lived alone)
meant darning thin socks
over a light bulb rather than buying new

for ten years he drove the same rusted truck
stopped smoking for the sole reason
that it cost too much
sold the rifles
he'd spend hours just to shine

it meant saving the old-age pension
tallying up the sums so carefully
adding and re-adding them
on the backs of used envelopes
he kept on the end table by his favourite chair

so many sacrifices
just to leave me this money
and i'd trade it all   every single cent of it
to have heard him say he loved me
one hug worth all this cash
i'm left here holding now
so hard it is   so cold

expert

i'm efficient with death   i know where to go
who to see   what to do with the body
i'm used to the hush of funeral parlours
the solemn properly sympathetic director
with his cold handshake   his offers of lukewarm coffee
i know the cost of caskets   how to write an obituary
all about the opening and closing of graves

i can make all the decisions that have to be made
how much food to have for the tea
what clothes to choose for the burials
grandma's pink skirt   mom's yellow dress
my brother needed new pants

i know how to tie up all the loose ends death leaves
cancelling them with my green bag of certificates
telephone numbers   blue cross   pension plans

i know how to handle the tributes   flowers   cards
the tears   what to reply when someone says they're sorry
what to say when they don't know what to say
i'm good at it by now   the closing down of lives

what my body knows

i saw my father today
in the grocery store parking lot

of course it wasn't really him
gone months now
just someone with his long stride
tan winter coat
much like the one he wore
blue jays ballcap
pulled low over his eyes
i nearly called out *dad*

i remember after marie died
driving past a woman
who turned to smile
and there she was
the same curled hair
same out-of-style glasses
i waved then realized

and david too   i saw him
everywhere at first
i cried each time
there was someone
too much like him

it is said we inhabit
nothing so much as loss
i have taken them inside me
these people
once so much part of my life

and even though
i realize they're gone
it's what my body knows
when reminded of them
when i say to myself
the sound of those lost names

part two

something
worth keeping

making a marriage

for years i thought there must be some recipe
i hadn't yet found   some certain ingredient
i must be missing and i made this marriage
the only way i knew   the way i was taught
to portion out love like small pinches of salt

i was doing it wrong (though i held in my hands
the bowl's smooth shape) making a well
in the centre   forgetting to put anything in

small wonder we fell in the middle
small wonder things seldom turned out

something worth keeping

if the television was gone
how would you pacify your need
to be anywhere but here

where would you go to escape
when fried green tomatoes is no longer
a movie but wednesday's lunch
and the remote is lost forever
down the cushions of the couch

would we begin with the silence
that has fallen between
the television's constant gabble
and all the words we never get to say

could we just change our channel
find something worth keeping
before the static returns
and the picture starts dimming
before we both end up turning away

frazil ice

like frazil ice
in fast-flowing rivers
battered about
and always
in danger
of being pushed under
broken apart
by the constant
pitch and toss
the wild
unsteady currents
your love for me
formed
on the open
and turbulent waters
the rapids
of my heart

*frazil ice: ice crystals or flakes formed in the turbulent
waters of rivers – Dictionary of Canadian English*

risks

the sign reads *riptides swim at your own risk*
the ocean some wild white beast
i watch you dive in
should know you'll be okay
you never take a risk
that isn't calculated

it's me who doesn't calculate
who never knows the risk worth taking
not able to measure levels of danger

how can you be so sure
the waves will wash you back
onto the safety of that shore
how do you decide in life
what isn't going to scare you

tell me how you measure
the risks your heart can handle
the risks your heart won't take

no warning

five minutes before
the floodgates open
a warning bell sounds

a great rush of water
cascades into the gorge
boils over rocks
dry riverbed

i come with no warning
you are caught
swept up
in the onrush
that leaves you
breathless floundering

i push you under
hold you there

durable goods

mother served us meals
on melmac plates
shatterproof and serviceable

rarely brought out
her good china
royal crown derby
blue mikado
so fine
when held to the light
you could see
right through

ringed with gold
and veined with faint tracings
of blue on milky white

delicate as mother's still hands
not durable enough
for everyday   too frail
for her children
to hold

       ....

i have thrown you
so many times
never saw you crack
not even once

thought you could withstand
almost anything i did
durable goods you were
tough as mother's melmac plates
as indestructable

how long you have lasted
loving me anyway
not breaking
not taking anything back
                ....

you need a woman
who can heft
forty pounds of flour
a good strong polish woman
like dad used to say
her feet firmly planted
in sensible shoes

a no-nonsense
kind of woman
who can bake bread
and build log cabins
all before lunch

a woman who can catch the day
in capable hands
make of it
exactly what she wants
it to be

  ....

mother's prized china tea set
american beauty
roses like the ones she grew
that twined about the trellis
in her garden

when she died
dad tore them up   replaced them
with something practical
carrots potatoes parsnips

he wanted those things
that would keep through the winter
things he could make last
        ....

women like my mother
like me
we are a different thing
with our fine wrists
our too sad eyes

we feel too much
break too easily
should be stamped *handle with care*
wrapped in bubble wrap

perhaps we are better left
a collection of bone china women
with old-fashioned names
like laurel or sarah
who sit atop undusted shelves
too fragile to be useful
too costly to ever touch

desires

there they are again
luna moths

that come to me
in moonlight

battering
against my body

their pale wings
whispering old wishes

in the softmouthed night

she is drawn to it
the way moths are drawn
to wander the night lost
in search of flame

that kind of desire she has
that owns you
each torn breath a surrender
that leaves you open
your whole body trembling

that kind of desire

it leaves her naked
on ashy wings
as she steps over and over
into her wanting

but such heat
she knows   such heat
in the softmouthed night

promises

my friend and i loll in the languid heat
of late july   dresses cling to our damp skin
we kick off sandals   wriggle bare toes in thick grass
watch as a wedding party gathers nearby
women in pastels   men in dark slacks
we pity the bride in her heavy gown
marrying here on a day too hot for anything

we are talking in the way only two women
who are unafraid of truth can   unafraid of that sharing
we talk about desire   how it has its way with us
how it sings along our skin   moves inside our bodies
like a heat wave   leaves us restless
always wanting something more

the air shimmers around us white and hot
as the summer sky   as the bride's satin dress
where she stands beneath a blaze of sun
making promises we know she really means to keep

what she must never do

at fifteen my first boyfriend
my mother saying *don't disappoint me*
she never once mentioned sex
but i knew what she was telling me

aunt may   my mother's sister
sent away at seventeen
to have the baby she would never know
mom remembering her father's fury
as may sat bent beneath the names
she'd never heard before

shame in his eldest daughter
burned so deep in every word
that my mother listening
knew what she must never do
do not disappoint me

the commandment her father gave
a lesson she learned and taught me
about the conditions there are to love

easier

*it is easier in our society to be naked physically than to be naked
psychologically or spiritually – Rollo May*

you have seen me
naked in my thoughts
more vulnerable
than if
i'd stood before you
and undone my clothes

i wish
it was my body
i had shared with you
my belly and my breasts

how much easier
that would have been
how much less naked
i'd have been to you
how much less
you would have known

those dark hours

the night gave away
so much
we would not reciprocate
kept the moon
only to ourselves
woke in the morning
exhausted
from keeping inside us
those dark hours

the rain held the night
its small dance
against our skin
cool as dawn
blue as wanting

there were no answers
in that night
the dark reflected
only questions

the moon was an apple
tempting us
but we would not
take a bite

incessant

as prairie wind tendrilling wild
through the dry dirt days
cracked skin of summer

you wandered my blue evenings
wove every winter dream
wind twisting inside me

a bruised sound
dark as a secret
staggering as love

something about last night

about forever and never
did you hear it too

something about last night
and the way
it ran into morning
like rain
runneling a windowpane

the way words
slur into sentences
whose meaning
we don't understand

something about last night
and the way your eyes
absorb me   pull me down

something about touching
with no hands
about truth about laughter
the lessons i'm learning
the love

something about last night
the hush of sky and stars
and knowing the small hours together

something about fingertips
about breath
about time and how little
there really is

going under

if i fall into you who will save me
if i drown in you am dragged down
by your mouth your eyes
if i go under caught up
in that swift whirlpool of wanting

what will be left of me
when not even i am there
to save me from myself

who will answer when i call
help me   please help me
when i cannot swim
the dangerous length of your body
high winds all around
and it's too deep and so cold

who will be there to find
my still and sunken heart

wish

place your thumb
firmly against my hipbone

wrap your fingers
around my thigh

my body is the wishbone

break me in half
see if i don't come true

more stone than water

it was more like no than yes   more an answer than a question
a truth you didn't really want to know   it was more like the stars
hung there in the black branches   their sharp points cutting my
skin   it was more dirty than clean   the ring around the bathtub
you need to scrub away the wet grounds in your coffeepot   more
like being emptied of anything resembling love   emptied like the
last drop in the orange juice pitcher   hollow as the mountain ash
we finally cut down   rotted through   it was more like something
lost   like taking off your clothes to find your body gone
evaporated into the night   or a friend who suddenly packs up and
leaves you a small book   the words meaning little now
untranslatable   it was more stone than water   a wound closing
over   more like something broken   a terrible fever in the darkened
corners of my room   it was more nothing than something   cheap
as those fake sapphire rings   the ones they sell at walmart   set on
foam squares in little blue cardboard boxes   that worthless

any day

give me no paperback lotharios
filled with pretty promises
empty as the silver shakers
stored on the back shelf
of my grandmother's china cupboard

give me always and any day
one good man
honest as salt
who means what he tells me

one man who loves
who lives and breathes
right here in the real world

his mouth moving hard on mine

laden

i can feel this weight inside of me
heavy as the split stones
the ones you brought home
from the churchill river
the ones i made a footpath of
between the flowerbeds of irises
and late september lilies

this weight in me as heavy
as it must have been for you
when you carried one by one
the burden of those stones
down the churning rapids of that river
just to bring them back for me
because i wanted them

this heaviness i know i bring to you
this weight you carry and carry for me always
laden with the split stone of my heart

in the small of the night

you wake me
something's wrong
my head on your chest
i listen to your heart beat
to no real rhythm

endless ambulance ride
the driver making talk so small
i cannot follow

intensive care waiting room
on the newly painted walls
a cross-stitch of the serenity prayer
framed in pink
on the table
someone here before me
has left a single white kleenex
folded over and over
into a very small
very perfect square

i must phone
to ask permission
to see you
for just ten minutes
at a time
i take a breath
go in smiling

i cannot think
senses confused
in my mouth
sound of your heartbeat
your breath in my eyes

home again
the storm has passed for now
we are learning a new language
cat scan arrhythmia
atrial fib
the names of medications
atenolol digoxin
now this latest
and most frightening
transient ischemic attack
a t.i.a. a warning

i try not
to think about this
try not to sleep
with my eyes open
but its always like this
if you survive the biggest storms

they don't seem real
you keep on watching
the sky forever

even when i pushed

away for a week now
repairing fire towers
i think of you there
working eighty feet up
nothing but sky and wind
stretched all around you

yet i am not afraid
i have pushed you higher
to far more dangerous edges
much steeper climes

even when
i conjured storms
that could have sent you
plummeting   you held on
even when i pushed
you would not fall

sixteen

i was lost in love   stayed up late listening to
forty-fives on the old red phonograph crooning
about moody river and its muddy waters

when you were gone i was sad as my mother's old bathrobe
languished on my bed nibbling the chocolates you'd sent
me from a ribboned box   i remember black magic

that long-ago summer when moonlight
slept in the spruce boughs   we slowdanced
the heat of the whole length of your body against
mine   the scent of woodsmoke mingled with the warm
taste of our wanting

small gestures

my words
are like smoke over water
sun motes
feathers on the wind
almost air   he tells me

it's actions
that mean something
what i do
not what i say

he does his reading
in my eyes
the slow language
of my body
the way i move

it's in my hands
my fingers
on the ridges of his collarbones
the way i turn
into his arms

it's in this tenderness
these small gestures
forget your words
he tells me
be to me
what you say i am

walls

i no longer want these walls
tired of all that's happened here

tired of the relentless shade
the closed confines of these too small rooms

our new home   filled with bright spaces
swept in the hues of water and sky

colours with names like *translucence*
blue yonder   summer lullaby

we'll paint these new walls
together we'll fill them all with light

starting over

i spend the afternoon
planting thirty white spruce trees

i dig and water   haul soil in the old snow shovel
enjoy doing this work
don't have to think   just do the job

new home   new yard
everything about this place a starting over

i tamp it all down   firming everything
to a new and a permanent place

part three

the scent

of snow

six steps

(for jack, who showed me)

be the last to blink

dive deep and stay under

pick up small stones
just for the sound of them

taste words
try murmur fontanelle crescendo

do not dance outside of any fire

touch the dark gently
take what it has to give

impatient

mother french-braided my hair
while i squirmed on the high kitchen stool
she pulled and tugged
admonishing me *for heaven sake lynda sit still*
i was impatient to be outside
to run across twenty-fifth street
to the michaels' house
where butchie and wanda and ronnie and i
would play kiss tag out back in the woods
i would trip
just so butchie would catch me
coming home my pink hair ribbon
tangled   grass in my braids
and my mother ready to straighten me all over again

the scent of snow

how can i persuade you
she is a dangerous woman

do not take her lightly
though she appears innocent
dressed as she is in white

but trust me
she is trouble
has a hunger in her
that knows no bounds
a blizzard
she comes   a white desire
obliterating everything

notice the scent of snow
in the air surrounding her
the way sleet ticks
at the corners of her eyes

keep your distance
i warn you
find some way around her
even her poems
hold the cutwork crystals
of her winter dreaming
the cold burning
of these january nights

self portrait

i wanted you to know me
thought in this way
you might see
how light only skims my surfaces
forehead   chin   bridge of my nose
like a pebble skips on water

hoped you might find me
deep in the alternation
of darkness and bright
caught there
in that continuous
shift of meaning

behind these bars
of shuttered sun
my eyes are the shadows
that speak of too much
for any light to ever hold

purple

i love the way it settles inside me
like some small pocket of night
sometimes it surrounds me
wraps me up so thick   so tight
i try to see out   i try
but the purple it just says no

there are times i think
i don't really love it
but i must or why would i leave myself
so open   inviting purple in

there are times i think it wants to own me
to keep me there among its shadows
breathing purple   tasting its flavour
hearing its dark song

cactuspoem

once poems sprang up
thick and fast
from some fertile place
where language flourished
lush and green
as the seven-foot ferns
growing wild
on the kingsmere trail

i live now
in a great sand hills
desert of words
among wolf willow
sagebrush
and dry scrub

only the occasional
tangled tumbleweed
the odd prickly cactuspoem

cocoon

at first the naked woman found herself shopping
for underwear   white cotton bras
in boxes with daisies on them
one size fits all pantyhose   natural beige

she's taken to wearing baggy brown pants
with elastic waistbands   grey turtleneck sweaters
extremely sensible shoes

the naked woman rather likes this new feeling
bundled to the neck   covered from head to toe
inside her cocoon of clothing

she can't feel any more the wind's sharp stinging
can't feel a thing in those places
that used to be once so bare

the dance

two steps forward   one step back   one step forward
two steps back and the dance isn't an easy one   it's hard oh it's hard
but there are days when i've got it and move to the music
i understand the rhythm and it's so smooth and elegant
i could do this forever   it's not really difficult at all
and i glide through my days

but then something happens   i can't remember a thing i've learned
not sure how to move my arms my feet   my thoughts tripping me
on the dance floor and i stumble and fall   awkward as a toddler
in her first pair of shoes and i sit there and wail
i wail like that small child   because just yesterday
i knew the steps   just yesterday i had it   and now
once again
it's gone

the clearing

your healing is not a straight line – Henri Nouwen

i hoped it would be
hoped i could read the book
take one pill once a day
and be fine forever
it would be all i'd need
to stop the damage that i've done

hoped this would bring an end to it
like calling in the backhoes
men with axes   to break a line
to keep the fire from spreading

praying that this time
the blaze won't leap
the clearing
that this time the flames
might be held back

it's time

to begin again
to lose all the old desires
old habits dying their hard deaths
time i arrived like a newborn
into the bright world

learned to be
the child i never was
make angels in a slow snow
chase sandpipers
along the summer shore

time i woke to shifting skies
to breakfast on plump strawberries
from a blue china bowl

to hold all i can
of all there is for me
to touch the whole day
touch each single shining minute

it's time i breathed the sun-warmed air
it's time i really breathed

to begin again

a tabula rasa
the slate swept clean

to have the past
written in soft pencil

i can simply erase
leaving the page pristine

to write the words
i could not find before
because i could not feel them

to say
what's there now
when i look at you

how my eyes begin
at last   to see

such sun

(for pat)

on my table
sits the mexican bowl
my sister brought back
from cancun
it holds a hundred colours
brilliant as mexico itself

beneath a cobalt sky
amber-skinned women
bear baskets of oranges
there are parrots
and coconut palms
whitewashed houses
with their red tile roofs
emerald fish swim
in an emerald sea

you are as happy to me
little sister
as that mexican bowl
as bright with colour
i can see you there
in that market
beneath those coconut palms
where you bought my bowl
hear you laughing
among the tall flames of flowers

when i see that bowl
i think always of you
moving so easily
into laughter
holding in your hands
such sun

at fifty

at fifty, according to Kong Zi, one becomes perfect
— from "Ingratitude" by Ying Chen

i'll wake each morning
my thoughts smooth as satin sheets
silvery as the mirror which reflects me
flawless   unwrinkled as my freshly pressed skirt

i'll breakfast on croissants
while reading in the morning sun
(i won't need glasses til i'm fifty-one)

i'll know what i want when i'm fifty
who i am   where i'm going
i'll be wise and wonderful   wacky and wild
my grandsons will tell me i rock

i'll be so fine when i am fifty
sophisticated as audrey hepburn
cultured as my grandmother's pearls
i'll be one of those women
whose very presence changes the quality of air
at fifty i'll finally have finesse

gathering light

these are the first
the fragile days
i gather light
in golden armfulls
and i am finding
that its everywhere
light spilling through my fingers
dancing in the branches
of the ornamental apple

too long i lived
in the wounded rooms
of my heart
too long in the absence of light
where all lost things gathered

these are the first
the fragile days
i wake now to bright mornings
your breath
warm on my neck
the sunlight slanting in

that i will turn gently

i walk the trail above the shell river
early september   an afternoon warm and slow as syrup
max snuffles his way ahead of me looking for squirrels
i gather leaves to press between the pages of heavy books
the colours are glorious   caramels lemon yellows
and raspberry reds

the old season ends   a hush here quiet as church
i come to listen to the old forest
it knows about patience and being still   about simplicity
knows my human heart is far too complicated   needs simplifying
time now to enjoy the frost-touched mornings
deer moving up from the river   geese in concert overhead

i say a prayer that the old season will end in me too
that i will open myself to this new season
as gracefully as does this forest
that i will turn gently as these leaves i hold
like small flames in the palms of my hands

part four

fire
_____
stories

a woman
leans into heat
and once again
she is caught

sparks the darkness
into fire

her eyes ripple
the blaze wavers
along her collarbones

swims the cool channels
of her body

owning her
    ....

gathered around an autumn fire someone tells the story
of the artist   who one evening partying on the beach
and lofty on wine   tripped face first into the fire
how when he fell he reached out   grasped the iron
ring set into the firepit   burned his hands so horribly
he could never hold the brush again   how he lived
regretting always that one misguided step   unable
to forget that one false move   his blackened hands
brushing ashes into the starless night

    ....

my father toasting marshmallows
when one caught fire
he flicked the willow spear
to put out the burning stickiness
and it flew stuck blazing to his forehead
left him branded
a small round scar
he told no one about

....

dougie sutherland sat in front of me in fifth grade
lived with his drunken parents   five brothers
and sisters in a wartime house with peeling yellow paint
the yard high with couchgrass and russian thistle
they said one night   his parents gone   the four-year-old
found matches   set the cluttered house ablaze

they said dougie was a hero
that he fought his way through the strangling smoke
to save the baby left in a crib on the upstairs floor
but what i remember most is the empty desk
in front of me   that dougie never came back to school

        ....

great fires create their own rules
their own weather
dangerous and beautiful
we are here to fight this fire
and here because to some humans
fire is irresistible

we are surrounded by fire
it rolls off the tops of trees
spins into the air
the forest a bright orange vapour
thirty storeys high
around us the rocks glow
the full moon fills with blood

burning branches blazing needles
sizzle down on us
we beat out embers on one another's backs
heat cracks our lips   dries our lungs

we fight fires
our lives sudden and changing
and beyond our control
out of control we feel free
we become fire

        ....

my grandson plays in the fire
i see how it mesmerizes him
more than his brothers
how he cannot keep away
despite the danger

how fire entices him
holds him
as it holds me
with an intensity
we can do nothing about

how he finds in the flames
a familiar hunger
a longing we recognize
something both of us understand
    ....

it was a terrible thing
she tells me
the way that fire just didn't care
stole the book by my bed
my babies' photos
even my panty drawer

had no respect for anything
that thief robbed me
left me a bag lady
this charred hole
where my life used to be
    ....

fire moves in you like morning
delicate and slow   flickers
sweet as a lover's tongue   beckoning
you to come   fire a temptress
delectable in her high heels
and crimson skirts   the rustle
of her soft voice
saying take me   take
me now

    ....

no rain for weeks now   back of the house the forest
is crackling dry   i am burning   raking leaves   dry grass
i am not watchful   the blaze escapes me   it spreads
so quickly   sweeps through the trees   vaults from branch
to branch   crowning the tops of pines   and i can't put it out
can't stop it   one solid red wall of flame   the fire leaps the river
soon the whole city   all the buildings   firemen everywhere
scream for people to run   run for their lives   but there are
those who won't leave   who stay inside and burn
the walls turning to honeycomb around them   and when
it's over i stand there   alone in the smoke and silence
and it's i who have done this   set fire to everything
and watched as the whole world burned

    ....

there was a time
a left-handed woman
was seen as a danger
an ill-omened opposite
shadowy with secrets

a left-handed woman
an enchantress
conjuring the dark
too suspect
there was a time
bound to the stake
she was burned for it

    ....

conflagration

how often do you watch a friend kiss a conflagration?
– R. Thompson

part your lips
for this kiss
feel its leap
hold the flame
in your mouth
a lover's tongue

to kiss a conflagration
is to listen to jazzmen
playing in jackson square
in the furnace heat of late summer
your skin slippery
clothes clinging to the backs of your legs

look into the eyes of the fire you are kissing
those eyes are whirlpools they draw you in
lust boiling over your body like lava

step into that circle of heat
and you will taste
roma tomatoes   pepper and garlic
red onions fried in butter
the air hot and moist

kiss a conflagration
and you will know
an agony of pleasure
the way a new lover
can introduce you
to your body all over again

the kiss traces your shoulders
licks the hollow of your throat
feel the burn as it blooms there
a small orange sun
this kiss that will burn through your body
burn you right down to your heart

Acknowledgements

The author would like to thank, as always, the members of sans nom poetry group, fine writers and dear friends all. Many thanks also to Glen Sorestad and the 2001 writer-in-residence program at Kenderdine Campus, Emma Lake. My gratitude also to my editor, Dave Margoshes, whose sensibility and encouragement helped me to hone this book. And much love to my family who believe I can write the moon down from the sky. Thanks for your faith in my writing and in me.

The following poems have appeared or are upcoming in the following publications:

"making a marriage" in *Amethyst Review*

several of the poems from "staring straight into the sun" in *Descant*

the entire suite "staring straight into the sun" was broadcast on CBC Radio, as were "when the moon slides" and "fire stories"

"something about last night" appeared in *Room of One's Own*

"more stone than water" in *Fiddlehead*

SCN television filmed readings of "durable goods," "staring straight into the sun," "when the moon slides," and "such sun" for the *Story Album* program

Several poems were part of collaborative gallery exhibitions with visual artists Gwen duda McBride and Lorraine Beardsworth

About the Author

Lynda Monahan is the author of one
previous collection of poetry, *a slow dance
in the flames*, published by Coteau Books.
She has had work published in a number of
Canadian literary magazines and has several
poetry sequences broadcast on CBC Radio
One. She teaches creative writing at the
Saskatchewan Institute of Applied Science
and Technology, Woodland Campus,
in Prince Albert, Saskatchewan and
facilitates writing workshops for school
groups and others.